YOUR INVITATION

· · · · · · · · · · · · · · · ·

YOUR INVITATION

• • • • • • • • • • • • • • •

AN 11-SESSION SMALL GROUP EXPLORATION
VIA DIALOG OF THE GOSPEL ACCORDING TO MARK

BASED ON THE BOOK, *THE INVITATION*, WRITTEN BY
JOHN DANNEMILLER AND IRVING STUBBS

ADAPTED FOR USE BY SMALL GROUPS BY
MICHELLE VAN LOON

The Invitation Study
© 2013, 2021 Living Dialog Ministries
PO Box 15125
Richmond, VA 23227

All Rights Reserved

Published in the United States of America by Living Dialog Ministries, a 501(c)(3) tax exempt organization. www.livingdialog.org

ISBN 978-0-9890791-2-9

Scripture quotations, unless otherwise indicated, are taken from the HOLY BIBLE NEW INTERNATIONAL VERSION.
Copyright © 1973, 1978, 1984, 2011 by International Bible Society. Used by permission of Zondervan. All rights reserved.

Cover and interior design by Frank Gutbrod

18 17 16 15 14 13 7 6 5 4 3 2 1

Printed in the United States of America

CONTENTS

INTRODUCTION 07

SESSION 1: Who is this man? [Mark 1:1–2:12] 12

SESSION 2: What is the invitation of Jesus? [Mark 2:13–3:30] 17

SESSION 3: What did Jesus say and do? [Mark 4:1–5] 22

SESSION 4: What does a disciple's life look like? [Mark 6:1–8:21] 28

SESSION 5: Why didn't they understand Jesus? [Mark 8:27–10:12] 34

SESSION 6: What do you want Jesus to do for you? [Mark 10:17–Mark 11:18] 41

SESSION 7: How did those in authority view Jesus? [Mark 11:19–12:44] 47

SESSION 8: Did the message of Jesus sound like anything people had ever heard before? [Mark 13:1–14:11] 54

SESSION 9: How did Jesus spend his last day with the disciples? [Mark 14:12–14:52] 59

SESSION 10: Was this the end of the road for Jesus? [Mark 14:53–15:39] 66

SESSION 11: How can an empty tomb contain an invitation? [Mark 15:40–16:20] 71

EPILOGUE 74

INTRODUCTION

During this eleven week study, we'll be exploring the New Testament book of Mark together, interacting with the dialog Jesus had with his followers and others. Our gatherings are for anyone who thinks Jesus is someone who might be worth getting to know better. If you have questions about what you've heard about Jesus or if you have questions you'd like to ask him, you'll find these gatherings especially interesting.

We'll be getting to know Jesus better and relating to one another through transforming conversation. Despite all the high-tech communications tools we have at our disposal, most of our usual communication is pretty shallow. We're conditioned to skim along the surface of ideas and events without discovering the profound truths that lie deep inside them.

Experiences are richer when they're shared, aren't they? If you took a trip to an exotic locale and saw things you'd never seen before, wouldn't you want to tell someone about it? Better yet, wouldn't you like to have someone along to share the "Wow!"?

In your small group of traveling companions journeying through Mark together, you can share your experiences through dialog. If you associate the word "dialog" with some dull and boring academic discipline, we invite you to a different understanding of the word. Dialog is the opposite of small talk: It is "big" talk, a kind of heart-to-heart sharing that has the power to transform everyone participating in the conversation.

Kinds of dialogs

There are different kinds of dialogs we'll experience during our gatherings:

- *Dialog with God* — We believe that God calls each of us to a relationship with him. This relationship gives meaning and purpose to our lives. God wants deep, personal and open communication with us.

- *Dialog with self* — As you eavesdrop on Jesus' conversations and spy on the events of his life, you may have thoughts and feelings that clarify, stretch and challenge your understanding of Jesus. You may think, "Did he really say that?", "I wonder what he meant by that?" or "I never thought about it that way before."

- *Dialog with others who are physically present* — The exchange of thoughts and feelings that amplify and deepen your understanding. Some of us learn of Jesus from the words of others.

- *Dialog with others who aren't present* — The words and ideas of others you've known interact with your own thoughts and shape your perceptions in both positive and negative ways.

Invitation to dialog

The kind of dialog we want to cultivate in our group is not another word for "discussion" or "debate." Discussion is analytical and typically picks things apart. In debate, sides seek to win points. Dialog, on the other hand, is a way for us together to seek understanding.

Author Louise Diamond explains that dialog is intended
- not to advocate but inquire
- not to argue but explore
- not to convince but discover

We listen to one another to find out what is meant. We assume that each member of the group has a piece of the answer to the question, and that together, the group can craft a new and better answer. We celebrate new insights, greater clarity, and deeper understandings when they occur.

Agreement is not the purpose of dialog. It is important to suspend judgment about others' contributions. Disagreements can be seen as a different way of looking at a subject. Disagreements can energize a group to seek meaning and clarity that goes beyond initial conflicting views.

How to use this guide

The eleven sessions in this guide will guide your group in dialog with Jesus and with one another through the New Testament book of Mark.

The guide couldn't be simpler to use. No advance preparation or study is required! Some groups may choose to begin each gathering with prayer, or take a few minutes to catch up on one another's lives.

To launch into your time of dialog, your facilitator or someone from your group will read a few brief paragraphs that are a mix of summary and direct quotation from the Bible. The direct quotations from the Bible are in *italics* in your text. Immediately following each section, you'll find a question or two designed to launch your group into dialog over the events and issues raised in the text. Your group should stop at the end of each session segment to consider the questions that are along side that part before moving onto the next segment of text. You'll find additional questions at the end of each session if your group is looking for further discussion or for personal reflection.

Plan on an hour or so for dialog for each meeting. Some groups have gone far beyond an hour due to the intensity and enjoyment of the dialog. Your group's facilitator should be sensitive to the time commitment each member has made to the group. Make sure those in the group agree to go beyond the stated time if extended discussion time seems to be warranted.

Remember that your group's facilitator is there not as an answer man or woman, but as a coach. Each member of your group brings insight and value to the dialog as you craft an answer together. Your facilitator will help to honor your group's time commitment and guide you through the material each week.

You'll close each session with dialog in prayer. Affirming that Christ has been with you as you've shared a meal and talked about his story each week is the foundation for this time. Members of your group may have needs in their lives or questions and concerns raised through the session's dialog. This guide offers some general tips about how to pray conversationally, as well as suggestions for how to shape your prayer experience. Prayer may not be a familiar discipline to you — but it can be as simple as dialoguing with a friend. And you are!

Each person must make his or her own decision whether to become a follower of Jesus or not. This decision has eternal implications. We hope and pray that as you and your group journey together with Jesus, with Mark as your guide, each member will be blessed, challenged and encouraged as you consider his invitation. Okay, let's get started with Session One—Who is This Man

SESSION 1

WHO IS THIS MAN?
Mark 1:1–2:12

A couple of decades after Jesus lived, his followers wanted to make sure that his story would carry on long after they were gone. Of the four retellings of Jesus' ministry found in the New Testament, many scholars believe that Mark's retelling of Jesus' ministry was written first. The whole story of Jesus told in the Gospel of Mark takes place in a country the size of the state of New Jersey over a period of just three years, but it changed the course of history — and continues to impact people today.

Mark's account begins with the preaching of John the baptizer, an unconventional character who spent most of his time in the wilderness. He wore clothing made of camel hair, and ate locusts and wild honey. He believed he was God's messenger, and his life's mission was to prepare the way for Jesus. John called people to repent

John baptized people in the Jordan River as a sign of their cleansing and renewal. One day, Jesus from Nazareth made his way to the Jordan and asked John to baptize him. In that moment, John was stunned as he realized that the man standing before him had nothing for which he needed to repent.[1] He said, in effect, *"I'm not worthy"*, but baptized Jesus anyway. When he did, a voice from heaven declared Jesus to be the beloved Son of God.

After this, Jesus headed into the wilderness for forty days to fast and pray. At the end of this period, he experienced intense temptation away from his mission by Satan, but emerged in Galilee proclaiming that the kingdom of God was at hand. He urged his hearers to repent and believe this good news.

[Mark 1:1-15]

- **Have you ever been told you need to repent? If so, how did those words affect you? Did you repent?**
- **What was the good news Jesus was preaching? Is it good news for you personally? Why or why not?**

Jesus chose to carry out his ministry through a small group of men he called *disciples* (which literally means "learners"). As he walked along the shores of the Sea of Galilee, he called two pairs of brothers at work fishing to come follow him. His invitation was compelling to these men. They responded by leaving everything and behind in order to follow him.

Jesus and his new followers went to a nearby town called Capernaum on the Sabbath[2] and entered the synagogue[3]. A man with an evil spirit entered the assembly and cried out,

---

1   To repent means you experience a profound change of mind, a turning of your will in a new direction, and a revamped purpose for living.
2   The Jewish Sabbath begins at sundown on Friday night and ends after sundown on Saturday night.
3   A synagogue was a place of assembly where people met for prayer, Scripture study and community gatherings.

"What do you want with us, Jesus of Nazareth? Have you come to destroy us? I know who you are — the Holy One of God!"

Jesus ordered the spirit to be quiet and leave the man. The unclean spirit convulsed the man and came out of him. Those gathered in the synagogue were amazed at Jesus' authority, and almost immediately, word began to spread about him.

He headed with his followers to the home of brothers Simon (also known as Peter) and Andrew. Jesus continued to amaze those around him as he healed Peter's mother-in-law of a fever. That evening, as if summoned to some great celebration, people began bringing those who were sick or possessed with demons to Jesus. He healed and freed many desperate people.

As Jesus and his followers began to travel around the region, he continued to perform miracles. News about him traveled like wildfire across a dry desert. As a result, Jesus could no longer enter a town openly but stayed outside in lonely places. Yet the people still came to him from everywhere.

[Mark 1:16–45]

- **Can you imagine dropping everything you are doing in order to follow a complete stranger? Do you think there was something about Jesus that attracted them? What might that have been?**
- **Why do you think Jesus chose to begin his ministry with healings and deliverances? What qualities did Jesus display in these miracles?**

When Jesus returned to the house at Capernaum, people packed out the house and surrounding yard. Four men attempted to carry a paralyzed man to him in hopes that Jesus would heal him. There was no way they could navigate his mat to get anywhere near Jesus, so they carried the man up onto the roof, opened a hole between the beams, and lowered him into the house.

When Jesus saw their faith, he said to the paralyzed man, "*Son, your sins are forgiven.*"

Not everyone took his bold pronouncement as good news. Some scribes, men who were experts in the law of Moses[4], considered what Jesus said as blasphemy[5] They believed only God could forgive sins.

Jesus responded, "*Which is easier: to say to the paralytic, 'Your sins are forgiven,' or to say, 'Get up, take your mat and walk'?*" He turned to the paralyzed man and said, "*Get up, take your mat and go home.*" The man did as Jesus said.

And the crowd was stunned by what they'd just witnessed.

[Mark 2:1–12]

- What impressed Jesus about the four men who brought their paralyzed friend to him? Do you have friends like this?
- What does their reaction to the event tell us about the scribes? What do you think they concluded from what Jesus said and did?

---
4 The Law of Moses is found in the first five books of the Old Testament.
5 Blasphemy is the crime of assuming to oneself the rights or qualities belonging to God alone.

FOR FURTHER DISCUSSION OR PERSONAL REFLECTION:

[MARK 1:1-15]
Mark's gospel records that an audible voice from heaven declared Jesus to be God's Son, and that Satan tempted Jesus in the wilderness. Do these supernatural happenings add or detract from this account? Why did Satan do this?

[MARK 1:16-45]
Do you think that what the Bible calls "unclean spirits" or "demon possession" exists in our day? Why or why not?

[MARK 2:1-12]
What does this event tell us about how Jesus saw himself?

What are your impressions of this account?

SESSION 2

WHAT ARE YOUR IMPRESSIONS OF JESUS?
Mark 2:13–3:30

During this session, we'll be following Jesus as his ministry shifts into high gear. He is gaining lots of followers with his dynamic words and miracles, but he's also making enemies.

Jesus and his small group of disciples returned to the shores of the Sea of Galilee. He saw a tax collector[6] named Levi sitting in his office and said, *"Follow me"*.

Levi walked away from his job in order to follow Jesus. When Jesus and his followers accepted Levi's invitation to dine in his home, a group called the Pharisees[7] questioned Jesus' judgment. How dare this young *religious leader* rub shoulders with tax collectors and sinners like Levi!

---

6 In those days, the job of tax collector was granted to the highest bidder. The "winner" of the job could charge whatever tax he wanted in order to cover — and exceed — his investment. The Jews in Jesus' day had to pay one-third of their income to the Roman government for taxes. Because they served as agents to the hated Roman Empire, many considered tax collectors traitors who were willing to sell out to the Roman overlords.

7 Pharisees were the ultra-observant branch of Judaism during the time of Christ. In addition to their reputation as the spiritual pacesetters of their day, Pharisees held a great deal of political power.

Jesus' response to their concern? *"It is not the healthy who need a doctor, but the sick. I have not come to call the righteous, but sinners."*

[Mark 2:13–17]

> ☐ **Have you ever sensed a call from Jesus to you? If so, how did you respond?**

One Sabbath, the Pharisees spied Jesus and his followers walking through a field, plucking and eating heads of grain as they went. The Pharisees challenged Jesus as they believed this act of *"work"* violated God's command to rest on the Sabbath. Jesus pointed out that King David and his companions had once entered the house of God and eaten bread reserved only for the priests. He added, *"The Sabbath was made for man, not man for the Sabbath. So the Son of Man[8] is Lord even of the Sabbath."*

A short time later, Jesus and his friends entered a local synagogue. The Pharisees watched suspiciously as Jesus invited a man with a shriveled, disfigured hand to come to him. Jesus looked at them and asked, *"Which is lawful on the Sabbath: to do good or to do evil, to save life or to kill?"* But they remained silent.

---

8   Son of Man was a title used throughout the Old Testament, most frequently to refer to a specific human being. Jesus refers to himself using this title in order to demonstrate both his humanity and his unique relationship with the Father.

Jesus bristled, grieved at their hardness of heart. He asked the man to stretch out his hand, and it was completely restored.

The Pharisees left and went to plot with the Herodians[9] on how to destroy Jesus.

[Mark 2:18–3:6]

> Why do you think the Pharisees wanted to destroy Jesus? What would their motives be?
>
> Have you ever seen people in our own day who "play the Pharisee" in the way they react to Jesus? Who? Why do you think they choose to behave this way?

Jesus withdrew to the Galilean hills for a brief respite and invited several others to follow him — and they did. He appointed twelve to be with him as his inner circle of apostles (which means *messengers*), also known as disciples[10]. Jesus sent his disciples out to preach the good news that God's kingdom had arrived in the neighborhood, and empowered them to cast out demons.

After calling the disciples, Jesus seized the moment to teach them a profound lesson about two subjects with eternal consequences — sin and the ministry of the Holy Spirit[11] — before he sent them out to preach. *"I tell you the truth, all the sins and blasphemies of men will be forgiven them.*

---

9 Herodians were members of a political party friendly with Herod, who claimed to be "King of the Jews".

10 Disciples were devoted pupils who followed a leader (in those days, a rabbi, or teacher) and car- ried on the teachings and practices of the master.

11 The Holy Spirit is the one who convicts people that they've broken God's laws and therefore need a Savior; the Holy Spirit points people to Jesus.

But whoever blasphemes against the Holy Spirit will never be forgiven; he is guilty of an eternal sin."

> ▪ What comes to mind when you hear the word "sin"? What is your view of sin? What do you believe is God's view of sin? Do you feel forgiven of all your sins? If so, why?

FOR FURTHER DISCUSSION OR PERSONAL REFLECTION:

[MARK 2:13-17]

Put yourself in Levi's place. How do you think you would feel about Jesus' invitation?

What do you find most striking about the calling of Levi the tax collector?

[MARK 2:18-3:6]

What did Jesus mean when he told the Pharisees, "The Sabbath was made for man?"

The Sabbath is meant to be a day set aside for rest. Do you observe the Sabbath? How? Why do you think it is important to do so?

[MARK 3:13-30]

About what do you believe Jesus charged the disciples to preach?

Does it surprise you that he gave them the power to cast out demons? Why?

Does it surprise you that Jesus referred to a sin that will never be forgiven? Why?

SESSION 3

WHAT DID JESUS SAY AND DO?

Mark 4:1–5:34

Though Jesus was attracting ever-larger crowds, his ministry was marked by all kinds of unusual encounters with desperate individuals. Each encounter was unique; each outcome brought greater understanding about the kind of kingdom to which Jesus was inviting people. But even his closest followers didn't always "get it".

When news about all that Jesus was doing got back to his family, they came looking for him. Jesus told those around him that anyone who sought to do God's will was his family.

He returned to the seaside, got into a boat and pushed out into the water in order to address the crowd that had gathered to hear him. He used parables[12] to paint a picture in his hearers' souls about the kind of revolutionary kingdom to which he was inviting them.

He told a parable about a farmer who went out to sow seed: "A farmer went out to sow his seed. As he was scattering the seed, some

---

12 Parables are simple stories crafted from everyday life that reveal profound truths.

fell along the path, and the birds came and ate it up. Some fell on rocky places, where it did not have much soil. It sprang up quickly, because the soil was shallow. But when the sun came up, the plants were scorched, and they withered because they had no root. Other seed fell among thorns, which grew up and choked the plants, so that they did not bear grain. Still other seed fell on good soil. It came up, grew and produced a crop, multiplying thirty, sixty, or even a hundred times." Then Jesus said, "He who has ears to hear, let him hear."[13]

[Mark 4:1–9]

> **What do you think Jesus meant when he said that whoever does God's will is his family? Do you feel part of God's family? Why? Why not?**

Jesus continued his teaching. *"Do you bring in a lamp to put it under a bowl or a bed? Instead, don't you put it on its stand? For whatever is hidden is meant to be disclosed, and whatever is concealed is meant to be brought out into the open."*

"Consider carefully what you hear," he continued. *"With the measure you use, it will be measured to you — and even more. Whoever has will be given more; whoever does not have, even what he has will be taken from him."*

That evening, as they were crossing the Sea of Galilee, a furious squall came up and whipped the sea into a choppy froth. Waves broke over the rails and the boat began taking on water. All the while, Jesus was sound asleep in the back

---

[13] Jesus explains the meaning of the parable to his disciples in Mark 4:13-20

of the boat. The terrified disciples woke Jesus and asked if he cared that they were all going to die. With a word, Jesus instantly calmed the storm and asked them, *"Why are you so afraid? Do you still have no faith?"*

They were terrified and asked each other, *"Who is this? Even the wind and the waves obey him!"*

[Mark 4:21–41]

> - Has there been a time in your life when you were afraid that something terrible was going to happen or that you were going to die? Describe that experience. What did that fear do to you? What did you do to overcome or relieve that fear?
>
> - What do you think Jesus meant when he related "fear" to "lack of faith"?

After another sensational episode where Jesus freed a man from the prison of demons in which the man had existed for a very long time, Jesus and his disciples arrived on the other side of the Sea of Galilee. A synagogue leader named Jairus met the group, fell at Jesus' feet and begged Jesus to come with him to his home to heal his dying twelve- year old daughter. While they were talking, word came to Jairus that his daughter had indeed died. Jesus brought his disciples Peter, James and John to Jairus' house. When they arrived, they found a sad commotion with people weeping and wailing.

Jesus entered the house and announced that the child was not dead, but merely asleep. Jesus took his disciples and the girl's parents, went in to the little girl and said, *"Little girl, I say to you, get up!"* Immediately, she stood up and walked around. Those present were stunned and amazed. In this case, Jesus charged them not to tell anyone what had happened.

[Mark 5:1-24, 35–43]

When Jesus and the others were on the way to Jairus' house, a woman who'd been bleeding for twelve years pressed through the crowd to try to get to Jesus. Despite spending all she had in search of a cure, she'd had grown worse over the years.

When she heard about Jesus, she came up behind him in the crowd and touched his cloak, because she thought, *"If I just touch his clothes, I will be healed."* Immediately her bleeding stopped and she felt in her body that she was freed from her suffering.

At once Jesus realized that power had gone out from him. He turned around in the crowd and asked, *"Who touched my clothes?"*

The disciples pointed out the obvious: they were surrounded by a large, anxious crowd. But Jesus kept looking around to see who'd done it. Trembling with fear, the woman told Jesus the truth.

He said to her, *"Daughter, your faith has healed you. Go in peace and be freed from your suffering."*

[Mark 5:24–34]

Though we often hear the cliché *Come on . . . step out of your comfort zone!*, it is often health concerns, relationship breakdowns or financial crisis that drags us out of that zone and into a place of desperation.

- Are you surprised that a religious leader like Jairus would come to Jesus with his plea? Why or why not? What power did Jesus display in this encounter? What does this encounter tell you about who Jesus is?

- Do you believe faith has the power to heal? Why or why not?

FOR FURTHER DISCUSSION OR PERSONAL REFLECTION:

[MARK 4:1-9]

What do you think Jesus meant when he said that whoever does God's will is his family?

As you consider the parable of the sower, what kind of soil is in your life — little soil, shallow soil, thorn-choked soil, or productive soil? Why? Is it possible to be a combination of some or all of them?

[MARK 4:21-41]

What is the lesson here about making wise use of God's resources in our lives?

[MARK 5:24-34]

Why do you think Jesus didn't want anyone to know about this?

Can you relate to this woman in some way? Have you ever felt as though you'd exhausted all options for solving a problem in your life?

Jesus took no credit for the woman's healing. Instead, he attributed her healing to her faith. What do you think was the source of her faith?

SESSION 4

WHAT DOES A DISCIPLE'S LIFE LOOK LIKE?

Mark 6:1–8:21

Jesus taught his disciples not only through their joyous successes in ministry, but also when their faith flagged . . . or failed. The journey with him exposed the doubts and struggles in their hearts in ways none of them could have ever anticipated the day he'd first called each one to follow him.

When Jesus and the disciples headed into Nazareth, the small town in which Jesus had grown up, they were received with bitter scorn. Many who knew him as a boy found him hard to believe. Something was happening in his life that made him seem very different than what he'd been before.

They left Nazareth, and Jesus decided to send out his followers in pairs to spread his message all over the region. He empowered them to represent him as they preached the need for repentance (change of heart and life direction), drove out demons from oppressed people and healed the sick. Jesus instructed them to travel light, taking no food, money or extra clothing with them, and encouraging them to stay with those who received them favorably.

News about Jesus and the ministry of his disciples spread, and King Herod, the ruler of Galilee in the north of Israel, caught wind of it. This is the same Herod who had ordered the beheading of John the baptizer. Rumors were circulating throughout the region about just who this Jesus of Nazareth really was. Herod took him to be John the baptizer raised from the dead. Others believed that he was one of the prophets of old, perhaps Elijah.

The words and works of Jesus' friends demonstrated the power of his message — a power that hadn't been seen in Israel since the time the prophets lived, hundreds of years earlier.

[Mark 6:1–29]

> Why do you think those who knew Jesus and his family in Nazareth were unable to accept him as he was now expressing himself?

When the disciples returned to Jesus after their journeys, they were overflowing with excitement about all they'd experienced. Jesus asked them to come away to a quiet place with him to continue to debrief, perhaps, and to rest.

But they didn't have much time to relax because word of the disciples' works had spread like wildfire. Droves of desperate people had tracked Jesus and the disciples to the remote place to which they'd stolen away alongside the Sea of Galilee. Jesus responded to the physical and spiritual hunger in the crowd as he performed a mass miracle, feeding 5000 people using just five loaves of bread and two fish. The crowd was immersed in a large-scale demonstration of God's creative power.

Afterwards, Jesus left his disciples and went alone into the hills to pray. By evening, the disciples had gone back out in the sea in their boat — perhaps to catch some fish. From the shore, Jesus could see his disciples struggling against the heavy winds. So he went to the disciples walking on the sea. The disciples were terrified. Jesus spoke to them saying, *"Take courage! It is I."*

He climbed into the boat with them and the wind died down. Their response to this series of events? They were completely amazed, for they had not understood about the loaves; their hearts were hardened.

[Mark 6:30–56]

> - What do you think it means to have a "hardened heart"? What would it mean to have a soft/receptive heart? Why is that important?
>
> - Given what they had recently experienced with Jesus, what can account for this hardening of the disciples' hearts?

Though Jesus and his disciples were Jewish, they did not adhere to the man-made traditions taught by Jewish religious leaders. When the Scribes14 and Pharisees asked Jesus why this was so, Jesus responded: *"Isaiah was right when he prophesied about you hypocrites; as it is written: 'These people honor me with their lips, but their hearts are far from me. They worship me in vain; their teachings are but rules taught by*

---

14 Scribes were responsible for creating perfect copies of the Old Testament Law. They also served as experts in the Law, interpreting for their people how the Law was meant to be expressed in every aspect of daily life.

men.' You have let go of the commands of God and are holding on to the traditions of men."

He further challenged the crowd watching this exchange to reconsider their ideas of purity: *"Nothing outside a man can make him 'unclean' by going into him. Rather, it is what comes out of a man that makes him 'unclean.'"*

[Mark 7:1–20]

> - **Based on this interchange between Jesus and the Pharisees, how do you think Jesus felt about religious traditions? What did Jesus mean by unclean?**
> - **What truth is Jesus teaching in this passage?**

Jesus then went into a non-Jewish village the scribes and Pharisees had insisted was off-limits and responded to an expression of faith in him by a Gentile woman by healing her daughter. As he journeyed from that village, he healed a deaf man who was unable to speak.

Though he asked people not to tell anyone about what they'd seen him do, word of these wonders spread rapidly. Crowds followed him into the remote regions in which he and his disciples were travelling. He performed another mass miracle, multiplying seven small loaves and handful of fish to feed more than 4,000 people.

In the wake of these dramatic events, the Pharisees approached Jesus and asked him to give them a sign from heaven. He told them no sign would be given to them and their followers. As Jesus and his disciples departed by boat, the group suddenly realized they had not brought along much food for their journey.

Still reflecting on his interchange at shore with the Pharisees, Jesus told the disciples to watch out for the leaven of the Pharisees and of Herod. Leaven (yeast) is a potent ingredient that causes dough to rise. His hearers understood leaven to be a spiritual picture of the permeating, transforming nature of sin. Jesus reminded them of the recent miraculous mass feeding and added, *"Why are you talking about having no bread? Do you still not see or understand? Are your hearts hardened? Do you have eyes but fail to see, and ears but fail to hear?"*

[Mark 7:24–8:21]

- What do you make of the disciples' lack of understanding?

- What do you make of Jesus' apparent frustration with their lack of understanding?

FOR FURTHER DISCUSSION OR PERSONAL REFLECTION:

[MARK 6:1-29]
What kind of power does Jesus give when he empowers people today? Is it of the same nature as this passage describes? Why do you say so?

[MARK 6:30-56]
After these events, what would you expect that the disciples would know to be true about Jesus?

How would you describe the relationship between Jesus and his disciples at this point in their journey together?

[MARK 7:1-20]
What was the main point Jesus was making about the practices of the Pharisees?

Jesus called the Pharisees and scribes "hypocrites". What did he mean by that?

[MARK 7:24-8:21]
Why did Jesus refuse to give the Pharisees a sign from heaven?

Do you see any parallels between the different ways people responded to Jesus in the accounts we've explored and the ways that you respond to Jesus? How so?

SESSION 5

WHY DIDN'T THEY UNDERSTAND JESUS?

Mark 8:27–10:12

For many generations, the Pharisees and scribes had relied on their strict observance of religious ritual to assure themselves (and everyone else) that they were in good standing with God. Jesus' words and works challenged this status quo. These religious leaders questioned Jesus about his motives and his identity at every turn.

But the Pharisees and scribes weren't the only ones who couldn't understand who he was or why he did the things he did. Even those who called themselves his friends didn't always understand his message.

Jesus asked his disciples, *"Who do people say I am?"* They told him that some thought he was John the baptizer raised from the dead, some others thought he was the prophet Elijah, and still others thought he was one of the other prophets. Jesus then challenged them: *"But what about you? Who do you say I am?"*

Peter exclaimed, *"You are the Christ!"*

When Peter responded, *"You are the Christ"* ("the Anointed One" in Greek), he was expressing confidence that Jesus was the Messiah, the King through whom the people of God would experience God's ultimate victory in history.

After urging the disciples to keep his identity to themselves, Jesus told them what lay ahead: He would be rejected by the elders, the chief priests, and the teachers of the law. He would ultimately be killed, and after three days, rise again. Peter, outraged at the very suggestion of such an end of Jesus' ministry, took Jesus aside and rebuked him for saying such things.

But Jesus silenced Peter: *"Get behind me, Satan!"* he said. *"You do not have in mind the things of God but the things of men."*

Jesus called together his disciples and the crowd that was following them to hear what he had to say next:

"If anyone would come after me, he must deny himself and take up his cross and follow me. For whoever wants to save his life will lose it, but whoever wants to save his life will lose it, but whoever loses his life for me and for the gospel will save it. What good is it for a man to gain the whole world, yet forfeit his soul?"

[Mark 8:27–38]

> - **If you were in Peter's shoes, how would you feel about Jesus' reprimand? Why?**
> - **What would it mean for you to take up your cross and deny yourself? What would it mean for you to lose your life for Jesus' sake?**

As Jesus and his disciples continued their journey, some of the disciples encountered a man casting out demons in the name of Jesus who had not been a part of their group.

At one point, when they imagined they were out of Jesus' earshot, the disciples quarreled about which one of them was the most important. When they arrived at their destination in the town of Capernaum, Jesus asked what they were arguing about. The group remained silent in response.

"If anyone wants to be first, he must be the very last, and the servant of all," Jesus said to them. He called a child to himself, took the little one in his arms, and said, *"Whoever welcomes one of those little children in my name welcomes me; and whoever welcomes me does not welcome me but the one who sent me."*

John then told Jesus about the man they'd met who had been casting out demons in his name, explaining that they'd told him to stop *"because he was not one of us."*

Jesus responded, *"Whoever is not against us is for us."*

[Mark 9:14–39]

> ■ **Jesus held the child before his disciples as a model of himself — welcoming a child is welcoming God. What is it about a child that puts an ego in proper perspective?**

Mark then reports a list of acts that would lead to grave consequences:

Whoever leads a child who believes in Jesus to sin . . . it would be better to have a great millstone hung round his neck and be thrown into the sea.

If your hand causes you to sin, cut it off . . . it is better to be maimed than with two hands go to the unquenchable fire of hell.

If your foot causes you to sin, cut it off . . . it is better to enter life lame than with two feet be thrown into hell.

If your eye causes you to sin, pluck it out . . . it is better to enter the Kingdom of God with one eye than with two eyes be thrown into hell.

Shortly after this conversation took place, when Jesus was in the midst of a spirited discussion with the Pharisees, people were bringing children to Jesus so he could touch and bless them. The disciples intervened and scolded these people — perhaps not wanting them to disturb his teaching. When Jesus saw what they were doing, he was indignant and said to them, *"Let the children come to me, and do not hinder them, for the kingdom of God belongs to such as these. I tell you the truth, anyone who will not receive the kingdom of God like a little child will never enter it."* And he took the children in his arms, put his hands on them and blessed them.

[Mark 9:42–10:16]

> **What does Jesus mean by receiving the Kingdom of God like a child? How can an adult receive the Kingdom of God like a little child? Have you done so?**

Jesus then invited Peter, James and John to come away with him into the mountains north of the Sea of Galilee. The three saw Jesus transfigure (change appearance). His clothes became dazzling white, and Old Testament figures Moses and Elijah joined him there. In the midst of this experience, a cloud surrounded the group, and a voice spoke: *"This is my Son, whom I love. Listen to him!"* Jesus asked Peter, James and John to keep this experience to themselves until after he'd risen from the dead. He knew that they would be able to better understand the power and meaning of what they'd witnessed when they'd experienced his resurrection.

> ■ **Ponder for a moment how the memory of this experience might have reshaped the way these disciples prayed in the years after these things happened. How might it impact your prayer life now?**

Jesus and his disciples traveled to the region of Judea beyond the Jordan River. Crowds flocked to hear Jesus teach. As usual, there were critics and skeptics mixed throughout the multitude. Some Pharisees put Jesus to the test with a question about whether it was lawful for a man to divorce his wife.

"What did Moses command you?" he replied.

They said, *"Moses permitted a man to write a certificate of divorce and send her away."*

"It was because your hearts were hard that Moses wrote you this law," Jesus replied. *"But at the beginning of creation God made them male and female. For this reason a man will leave*

his father and mother and be united to his wife and the two will become one flesh. So they are no longer two, but one. Therefore what God has joined together, let man not separate."

When the disciples asked Jesus to elaborate on this, he said that anyone who divorces and remarries commits adultery.

[Mark 10:1-12]

> Jesus made clear his position clear on marriage and divorce. Is there anything you would like to ask him about this? What would that be? Given everything you know about Jesus, how do you think he would respond to your question?

FOR FURTHER DISCUSSION OR PERSONAL REFLECTION:

[MARK 8:27-38]
When Jesus questioned his friends about his identity, Peter's response was "You are the Christ". If you said, "Jesus is the Christ", what would you mean by it? Would you be hesitant to make such a statement? If so, why?

Why do you suppose Jesus charged his disciples to keep his identity secret?

[MARK 9:14-39]
If you had been there among the disciples when they were discussing who was the greatest, what would you have said to them?

[MARK 9:42-10:16]
Jesus painted vivid pictures of the consequences of yielding to temptations. What do these words mean to you?

What does it mean to you when you hear Jesus say that it is better to cut off your hand than to risk hell? What kinds of behaviors might Jesus be referring to?

[MARK 10:1-12]
How do you think Jesus would respond to a divorced person who came to him? To a divorced person who was remarried? To a person who was divorced and remarried more than once?

SESSION 6

WHAT DO YOU WANT JESUS TO DO FOR YOU?

Mark 10:17–Mark 11:18

In this session, we'll listen in on Jesus as he continued to emphasize the counter-cultural nature of his mission with both his clarifying words and his healing ministry, and follow him into Jerusalem. Though no one traveling with Jesus realized it at the time, as the group of disciples and followers turned south to the Holy City, they were heading toward a showdown like the world had never before experienced.

After Jesus emphasized that only those with the simple faith of a little child could become a part of the kingdom of God, a man desperate to be a part of this kingdom ran up to Jesus and asked what he must do to inherit eternal life. Jesus reminded him of the Ten Commandments. The man responded that he had kept all of them since he was a boy.

"One thing you lack," he said. "*Go, and sell everything you have and give to the poor, and you will have treasure in heaven. Then come, follow me.*" At this the man's face fell. He went away sad, because he had great wealth.

Jesus then said to his disciples: *"How hard it is for the rich to enter the kingdom of God!"* The disciples were amazed at his words. Jesus added this: *"It is easier for a camel to go through the eye of a needle than for a rich man to enter the kingdom of God."* The disciples were even more amazed and asked: *"Then who can be saved?"* Jesus looked at them and said, *"With man this is impossible, but not with God. All things are possible with God."*

[Mark 10:17–31]

> ■ **Many who lived during the time of Jesus equated riches with God's blessing. What is the message of Jesus to the man who possessed great wealth? Do you think this means those who are wealthy can not be saved?**

Two of the disciples, brothers James and John, returned to a topic that had frequently come up among the group when they asked Jesus for important positions next to him in glory. *"You don't know what you are asking,"* Jesus told them. *"Can you drink the cup I drink or be baptized with the baptism I am baptized with?"* Jesus told the pair it was not his role to assign seating in God's kingdom.

When the other disciples heard this, they became angry with James and John. But again Jesus reminded all of them, *"Whoever wants to become great among you must be your servant and whoever wants to be first must be slave to all. For even the Son of Man did not come to be served, but to serve, and to give his life as a ransom for many."*

[Mark 10:32–45]

> What is your view about 'status' in God's kingdom? How does your view square with the ideals of our culture?

Jesus and his disciples next traveled to Jericho where Bartimaeus, a blind beggar, shouted *"Jesus, Son of David, have mercy on me!"* as the group and a large crowd following them passed him on the road out of the city. Those nearby rebuked him and told him to be silent, but he cried out with even more intensity. Jesus stopped and called for the man. *"What do you want me to do for you?"* Jesus asked.

The blind man said, *"Rabbi, I want to see."*

"Go," said Jesus. *"Your faith has healed you."* Immediately the man received his sight and began following Jesus.

[Mark 10:46–52]

> If Jesus were here right now and asked you, "What do you want me to do for you?" how would you answer?

Jesus and the disciples came to the towns of Bethphage and Bethany at the Mount of Olives, on the outskirts of Jerusalem. Jesus sent two of his disciples ahead to locate a colt that had never been ridden tied up in the next village. *"If anyone asks you, 'Why are you doing this?' tell him, 'The Lord needs it and will send it back shortly.'"*

They did as they were told and got the response Jesus predicted. Jesus rode the animal into Jerusalem as a crowd lined the route to welcome him. Some people threw their cloaks across the road before him, and others spread branches they'd cut in nearby fields. The throng was shouting *'Hosanna! Blessed is he who comes in the name of the Lord! Blessed is the coming kingdom of our father David!"*

[Mark 11:1–11]

> **How would you describe the crowd's behavior? Their expectations of Jesus?**

Jerusalem was crowded with Jewish pilgrims who'd come to the holy city for the Passover festival. All male Israelites were required to pay a tax to the Temple with special coins. People who came from far-off places needed to have their native currency converted into the currency used at the Temple. Those who converted the currency were called *moneychangers*, and some levied a hefty surcharge for the service. Those who wanted to worship at the Temple were also required to purchase sacrificial animals from the Temple merchants who sold them at a steep margin.

When Jesus entered the Temple, he overturned the vendors' tables and exclaimed, *"Is it not written, 'My house will be called a house of prayer for all nations?' But you have made it a den of robbers!"*

When the chief priests and scribes heard about this, they began plotting in earnest to destroy Jesus. They feared him because the crowds of common people were buzzing in amazement about his teaching, and because he had *profaned* the Temple and its worship.

[Mark 11:12–18]

> Who is Jesus confronting here? Why? Do you think this confrontation squares with what most people think about Jesus?

FOR FURTHER DISCUSSION OR PERSONAL REFLECTION:

[MARK 10:17-31]

What would it have taken for the wealthy man to follow Jesus?

What does Jesus mean by his words "with God all things are possible"?

[MARK 10:32-45]

What is the role of competition in a "last shall be first, least shall be greatest" society?

[MARK 10:46-52]

How would you describe your faith? Do you think there is any difference between belief and faith? Why or why not?

[MARK 11:1-11]

In that day, Romans soldiers and foreign dignitaries made dramatic entries into Jerusalem with all the fanfare of royalty. Does this ride on colt-back seem to you to be the kind of entry appropriate for someone inviting citizenship in the Kingdom of God? Why or why not?

[MARK 11:12-18]

To what extent do you think that the religious leaders in charge of the Temple were sincere in their management of the Temple?

If you saw some religious leaders taking advantage of people seeking God, would you be willing to stand up to them? Why or why not?

SESSION 7

HOW DID THOSE IN AUTHORITY VIEW JESUS?

Mark 11:19–12:44

When Jesus and his followers arrived in Jerusalem to celebrate the Jewish festival of Passover, the long-simmering tensions between Jesus and the religious leaders heated to a boiling point. In this session, we'll explore some of the "hot button" issues drew Jesus into growing conflict with this group of powerful men.

When Jesus and the disciples arrived at the Temple, those in power — the chief priests, scribes and elders — came together to challenge Jesus. They wanted to know where he'd gotten the authority for his words and actions, since they hadn't given it to him. At the conclusion of this verbal confrontation, Jesus told them this story:

"A man planted a vineyard. He put a wall around it, dug a pit for the winepress and built a watchtower. Then he rented the vineyard to some farmers and went away on a journey. At harvest time he sent a servant to the tenants to collect from them some of the fruit of the vineyard. But they seized him, beat him and sent him away empty-handed. Then he sent another servant to them; they struck this man on the head and treated him shamefully.

He sent still another, and that one they killed. He sent many others; some of them they beat, others they killed.

"He had one left to send, a son, whom he loved. He sent him last of all, saying, 'They will respect my son.'

"But the tenants said to one another, 'This is the heir. Come, let's kill him, and the inheritance will be ours.' So they took him and killed him, and threw him out of the vineyard."

Jesus went on to say that in the end, the vineyard owner would execute justice on the rebel tenants. The priests, scribes and elders understood that Jesus viewed them as the tenants in this parable. But they were afraid of the crowd, so instead of responding, they walked away from him, ending the conversation.

[Mark 11:19–12:12]

> **What might it look like to welcome the son into his vineyard in this parable? Who is the vineyard owner? The heir?**

The spiritual leaders in Jerusalem were determined to find a reason to have Jesus arrested. A group of them came to Jesus and said, *"Teacher, we know you are a man of integrity. You aren't swayed by men, because you pay no attention to who they are; but you teach the way of God in accordance with the truth. Is it right to pay taxes to Caesar or not? Should we pay or shouldn't we?"*

Jesus knew their hypocrisy. *"Why are you trying to trap me? Bring me a denarius and let me look at it."* They brought the coin, and he asked them, *"Whose portrait is this? And whose inscription?"*

"Caesar's," they replied.

Then Jesus said to them, *"Give to Caesar what is Caesar's and to God what is God's."*

Jesus again outsmarted those who attempted to make him seem like a heretic. In spite of the apparent support of the multitude that believed that Jesus was someone special, the religious leaders persisted in their efforts to destroy Jesus.

[Mark 12:13–17]

- **If Jesus was a threat (as the religious leaders obviously believed he was), what was at risk? Who was in jeopardy?**
- **What things belong to God? What does it mean to give to God what is God's? What does it mean to give to Caesar what is Caesar's?**

The chief priests, scribes, elders and Pharisees had taken their shots at Jesus — confronting him about various matters such as why his disciples ate with ceremonially unwashed hands and why he violated the Sabbath by healing sick people on Saturdays. Next, another group called the Sadducees came to challenge Jesus. They presented him with a hypothetical situation:

"Moses wrote for us that if a man's brother dies and leaves a wife but no children, the man must marry the widow and have children for his brother. Now there were seven brothers. The first one married and died without leaving any children. The second one married the widow, but he also died, leaving no child. It was the same with the third. In fact, none of the seven left any children. Last of all, the woman died too. At the resurrection whose wife will she be, since the seven were married to her?"

After declaring they knew neither the Scriptures nor the power of God, Jesus responded, *"When the dead rise, they will neither marry nor be given in marriage; they will be like the angels in heaven. Now about the dead rising — have you not read in the book of Moses, in the account of the bush, how God said to him, 'I am the God of Abraham, the God of Isaac, and the God of Jacob'? He is not the God of the dead, but of the living. You are badly mistaken!"*

[Mark 12:18–27]

> What are your thoughts about the resurrection of the dead? Do you believe in an afterlife? Why or why not?

Noting how deftly Jesus answered his challengers, one of the teachers of the law approached him and asked which of the commandments was the most important[15].

"The most important one," answered Jesus, *"is this: 'Hear, O Israel, the Lord our God, the Lord is one. Love the Lord your God with all your heart and with all your soul and with all your mind and with all your strength.' The second is this: 'Love your neighbor as yourself.' 'There is no commandment greater than these."*

Religious leaders of Jesus' day believed it was possible to love God without necessarily caring about other people. The teacher of the law agreed with Jesus, and added that obeying these two commandments was better than all the burnt offerings and sacrifices prescribed by the law to obtain God's forgiveness. Jesus told this wise man that he was not far from the kingdom of God. Jesus' answer to the man was astounding as he used a word for 'love' that applies to our will, not our emotions.

Jesus then told his disciples and the masses that the public shows of *righteousness* put on by the religious authorities were anything but righteous.

[Mark 12:28–40]

> - **What does it mean to love ourselves?**
> - **Is it possible to love God and not our neighbors? Why or why not?**

---

15 We might assume that this teacher was asking Jesus which of the Ten Commandments was most important. In fact, the man was asking Jesus about the list of 613 commandments in the Law, found in the first five books of the Old Testament. 248 were positive (things you should do) and 365 were negative (things you should not do).

At the conclusion of these exchanges with the religious leaders, Jesus sat down near the place where the financial offerings were collected in the Temple. Many rich people threw in large amounts. But a poor widow came and put in two very small copper coins, worth only a fraction of a penny. Jesus told his disciples that her gift was of greater value than the gifts of all the others because out of her poverty, she gave all she had to live on.

[Mark 12:41–44]

- What does this account tell you about the widow's values? What did she value? What was her view of God?
- How would you compare your own to hers?

FOR FURTHER DISCUSSION OR PERSONAL REFLECTION:

[MARK 11:19-33]
Why do you suppose Jesus was not more willing to discuss the source of his authority to the religious leaders?

[MARK 12:1-12]
As you reflect on this story, can you think of people in your life who have served in some way as God's messengers to you? Have you welcomed them? Or chased them away?

If you desire to serve Christ, that desire may mean that you'll experience the same kind of treatment the vineyard owner's servants did. What are your thoughts about this statement?

[MARK 12:13-17]
Why were the religious leaders so adamant in their efforts to get rid of Jesus?

[MARK 12:18-27]
What do you think God meant when he told Moses: I am the God of Abraham, the God of Isaac, and the God of Jacob?

What do you think Jesus meant when he said, "God is not the God of the dead, but of the living?"

[MARK 12:28-40]
Do you agree with Jesus and this scribe about what religious rules/commandments are most important to obey?

What do you think led (and continues to lead) religious leaders to behave as the Pharisees, Sadducees, elders, priests and scribes did toward Jesus?

SESSION 8

DID THE MESSAGE OF JESUS SOUND LIKE ANYTHING PEOPLE HAD HEARD BEFORE?

Mark 13:1–14:11

Though Jesus' life and ministry is often referred to as "good news", he didn't promise his followers a pastel-colored Candyland existence. There is a sobering final reality to his message. In today's session, we'll look at his explanation of the end of his story (and ours), as well as one person's unconventional response to his words and work.

Jesus and his disciples had spent time talking with the crowds and the religious leaders in and around the Temple in Jerusalem. As they left the holy city to return to their lodgings on the nearby Mount of Olives, one of the disciples called their attention to the magnificent buildings constructed of massive stones. *"Do you see all these great buildings?"* replied Jesus. *"Not one stone will be left on another; every one will be thrown down."*

Some of the disciples asked Jesus to clarify the signs that would signal the coming of the *"last days"*. He responded, *"Many will come in my name, claiming, 'I am he,' and will deceive many. When you hear of wars and rumors of wars, do not be alarmed. Such things must happen, but the end is still to come. Nation will rise against nation, and kingdom against kingdom. There will be earthquakes in various places, and famines. These are the beginning of birth pains."*

[Mark 13:1–5]

- **Do you see evidence of "birth pains" today? If so, what?**

Jesus told his disciples that the end of times would not come until the gospel was preached in all nations. They would be the agents through which this mission would be accomplished. He warned them that they would pay a price for associating with him: They would be betrayed, hated, beaten and taken to court, but he promised them that his Holy Spirit would supernaturally equip and empower them to respond to this opposition. *"All men will hate you because of me, but he who stands firm to the end will be saved."*

Jesus went on to say that the *"abomination that causes desolation"* would stand in a place where it didn't belong. Though we aren't entirely sure to who or what Jesus was referring, we do know that this abomination that causes desolation wreaks an unimaginable amount of destruction. Jesus offers the disciples the following instruction for enduring these difficult days until the end:

- Be ready to flee Jerusalem and head to the nearby mountains.
- Don't attempt to take your possessions with you
- This season will be especially hard on pregnant women and new moms; pray these days don't take place during the winter.

- Nothing like this has ever happened before — and it is for the sake of the ones chosen to follow him that this time of testing will be kept short.

- False prophets and messiahs doing signs and miracles will appear in order to deceive true followers.

- The sun, moon, stars and other heavenly bodies will go dark or be shaken from their fixed positions in the sky — and the Son of Man will come to gather and save his chosen ones.

Jesus concludes by telling the disciples *"No one knows about that day or hour, not even the angels in heaven, nor the Son, but only the Father. Be on guard! Be alert! You do not know when that time will come."*

[Mark 13:9–37]

- **What would you like to ask Jesus about these things? Does the Bible give any clues as to what this " abomination" might be? (Hint: See Daniel 9:27)**

- **Jesus clearly said that no one knows the date or time when the Son will come with great power and glory. What do you make of those who are willing to set the day and time for his coming? Do you believe Jesus is coming again? Why? Why not?**

After this, Jesus and the disciples were having a meal at the home of a man known as Simon the Leper in the village of Bethany on the Mount of Olives. A woman carrying a jar of expensive perfume interrupted the gathering in order to pour the contents of the jar on Jesus' head.

Some of those present were saying indignantly to one another, "*Why this waste of perfume? It could have been sold for more than a year's wages and the money given to the poor.*" And they rebuked her harshly.

"*Leave her alone,*" said Jesus. "*Why are you bothering her? She has done a beautiful thing to me. The poor you will always have with you, and you can help them any time you want. But you will not always have me. She did what she could. She poured perfume on my body beforehand to prepare for my burial. I tell you the truth, wherever the gospel is preached throughout the world, what she has done will also be told, in memory of her.*"

After this incident, one of the disciples, Judas, went to the chief priests in order to betray Jesus. They were delighted with this development, and promised Judas some money as a reward. Judas began watching for an opportunity to hand Jesus over to them.

[Mark 14:1–11]

> **What do you think could have led Judas to betray Jesus? Have you ever experienced betrayal? If so, can you briefly describe the experience?**

FOR FURTHER DISCUSSION OR PERSONAL REFLECTION:

[MARK 13:1-5]

How do Jesus' words on the last days strike you? Do you find them somber? To what extent do they concern you or make you think about how to live your life?

[MARK 13:9-37]

Where do you think false prophets and false saviors gain the power to perform signs and miracles?

[MARK 14:1-11]

Was the expensive perfume wasted? Why do you think on this occasion Jesus didn't "buy" the argument that proceeds from the sale of the perfume could have been given to the poor? (It is interesting to note that in the account of this event found in John 12:1-11, the one who objected most loudly was Judas, who served as the treasurer of the disciples.)

Jesus told his disciples that "wherever the gospel is preached throughout the world, what she has done will also be told, in memory of her." Why do you think that Jesus linked the act of this unnamed woman with the preaching of the gospel?

SESSION 9

HOW DID JESUS SPEND HIS LAST DAY WITH THE DISCIPLES?

Mark 14:12–14:52

It is hard for most of us to imagine how quickly things changed for Jesus during his last days in Jerusalem. When he entered the city, he was greeted as a hero. But within days, one of his closest followers betrayed him and rest abandoned him.

Though the geographical distance from Passover table to his middle-of-the-night "trial" is very short, each step of this day's events marks the longest journey of Jesus' life.

On the first day of the Passover observance, Jesus sent two of the disciples into the city, instructing them to follow a man carrying a jar of water until he reached his destination. Jesus told them to ask the owner of that house where he and his disciples could gather for the special Passover meal. He said the home's owner would direct them to a large furnished upper room ready and waiting for them. The pair followed Jesus' instructions and prepared the food and wine for the meal.

As Jesus and the disciples were eating the Passover meal that evening, Jesus said, *"I tell you the truth, one of you will betray me — one who is eating with me."*

His statement saddened the group, and each asked him, "*Surely not I?*"

He affirmed that it would be one of the Twelve, and continued, "*The Son of Man will go just as it is written about him. But woe to that man who betrays the Son of Man! It would be better for him if he had not been born.*"

[Mark 14:12–21]

> ■ **Knowing that Judas would betray Jesus, why would Jesus keep Judas around?**

Wine and unleavened bread had always been an essential part of the Passover meal for hundreds of years, but Jesus took these symbols and infused them with new meaning at the Passover meal he shared with the disciples in the upper room. Jesus took bread, gave thanks and broke it, and gave it to his disciples, saying, "*Take it; this is my body.*" Then he took the cup, gave thanks and offered it to them, and they all drank from it. "*This is my blood of the covenant, which is poured out for many,*" he said to them. "*I tell you the truth, I will not drink again of the fruit of the vine until that day when I drink it anew in the kingdom of God.*" They concluded the Passover meal in the traditional way — by singing a hymn.

After the meal, they returned to the Mount of Olives. Jesus told them that all of them would fall away from him, quoting an Old Testament prophecy: "*For it is written: 'I will strike* the shepherd, and the sheep will be scattered.' But after I have risen, I will go ahead of you into Galilee."

Peter declared, *"Even if all fall away, I will not."*

"I tell you the truth," Jesus answered, *"today — yes, tonight — before the rooster crows twice you yourself will disown me three times."*

But Peter insisted emphatically, *"Even if I have to die with you, I will never disown you."* And all the others said the same.

[Mark 13:22-37]

> **Why do you think Jesus attached such importance to this Passover meal?**

Later that evening, they went out to nearby Garden of Gethsemene. Jesus asked the disciples to wait while he went to pray. He took Peter, James and John with him and told them of his great distress.

Going a little farther, he fell to the ground and prayed that if possible the hour might pass from him. *"Abba , Father,"* he said, *"everything is possible for you. Take this cup from me. Yet not what I will, but what you will."*

He came back and found the disciples asleep. He asked Peter and the others, *"Could you not keep watch for one hour?"* He urged them to watch and pray so that they wouldn't be vulnerable to temptation. Twice more during the long night, this scene repeated itself.

Returning the third time, he said to them, *"Are you still sleeping and resting? Enough! The hour has come. Look, the Son of Man is betrayed into the hands of sinners. Rise! Let us go! Here comes my betrayer!"*

[Mark 14:32–42]

> ■ What does the Gethsemane experience reveal about Jesus' identity and his relationship with God? What strikes you most about his prayer?

Led by Judas, a crowd sent by the religious leaders and armed with clubs and swords entered the garden. Now the betrayer had arranged a signal with them: *"The one I kiss is the man; arrest him and lead him away under guard."* Going at once to Jesus, Judas said, *"Rabbi!"* and kissed him. The men seized Jesus and arrested him.

One of those standing with Jesus drew his sword and sliced off the ear of one of the high priest's servants. *"Am I leading a rebellion,"* said Jesus, *"that you have come out with swords and clubs to capture me? Every day I was with you, teaching in the temple courts, and you did not arrest me. But the Scriptures must be fulfilled."* Then everyone deserted him and fled.

[Mark 14:43–52]

> ■ Did it surprise you that each one of the disciples fled? Why do you say so? What might you have done if you were in their position?

After Jesus was arrested in the middle of the night, Peter (and perhaps, some of the others) followed him, warming himself near a fire in the large courtyard of the high priest's home. A servant girl said to him, *"You also were with that Nazarene, Jesus."*

Peter quickly denied it. The girl insisted that Peter was one of *them*. Peter told her he didn't understand what she was talking about and walked away to join another group huddled in conversation. Some of them noted his Galilean accent and insisted that he was with Jesus and the other disciples.

Peter responded with anger, calling down curses on himself, and he swore to them, "I don't know this man you're talking about."

Immediately the rooster crowed the second time. Then Peter remembered the word Jesus had spoken to him: *"Before the rooster crows twice you will disown me three times."* And he broke down and wept.

[Mark 14:66–72]

Peter's denial tells us something about how quickly courage and resolve can melt in the face of a challenge. Though Peter had insisted he would follow Jesus anywhere, he'd fallen asleep in the Garden three times after Jesus had begged the disciples to keep watch in prayer with him — and he'd denied ever knowing Jesus just hours afterward.

And yet, none of this was a surprise to Jesus. He knew exactly what his friends were made of — and he chose them anyway. He also knew that Peter's denial that night was not on the same murderous level as Judas' betrayal. Jesus knew that as Peter discovered exactly what Peter was (and wasn't!) made of, forgiveness would transform Peter from denier to unstoppable proclaimer. Peter's failure was not the end of his story.

> ■ **Have you ever denied knowing Jesus? If so, under what circumstances? How did you feel afterwards?**

FOR FURTHER DISCUSSION OR PERSONAL REFLECTION:

[MARK 14:12-21]

What do you think enabled Jesus to anticipate the arrangements provided for the Passover meal?

How do you think Jesus knew about his betrayal beforehand?

[MARK 13:22-37]

If you had been present at this Passover meal, what emotions might you have experienced? Why do you say so?

Do you believe that Peter and the others were absolutely sincere in declaring his loyalty to Jesus? Why or why not?

[MARK 14:32-42]

What might account for the lack of discipline on the part of Peter, James and John regarding Jesus' request for them to watch while he prayed?

SESSION 10

WAS THIS THE END OF THE ROAD FOR JESUS?

Mark 14:53–15:39

Jesus' journey leads him from a table surrounded by friends to two hurried trials to a place of torture and execution just outside of the city of Jerusalem. He went to a place of suffering and isolation in order to save each one of us from ever having to travel there ourselves.

After Judas betrayed Jesus in the middle of the night, his captors led Jesus to a place where the high priest, the chief priests, elders and teachers of the law had assembled. Many testified falsely against Jesus, but their statements did not agree.

The high priest conducting the trial asked Jesus, *"Are you not going to answer? What is this testimony that these men are bringing against you?"*

Jesus remained silent.

Again the high priest asked him, *"Are you the Christ, the Son of the Blessed One?"*

"I am," said Jesus. *"And you will see the Son of Man sitting at the right hand of the Mighty One and coming on the clouds of heaven."*

At this point, the high priest tore his garments — expressing his outrage — and asked what further evidence against Jesus was necessary, insisting that Jesus was guilty of blasphemy. The entire group agreed, condemning Jesus as worthy of death. Some spat on him, others beat him, attempting to humiliate him by blindfolding him and challenging him to prophesy.

[Mark 14:53-65]

> - If you were appointed counsel to represent Jesus in the trial, what argument would you have made for his innocence?
> - Do you think any argument — however brilliantly conceived and skillfully presented — could have swayed the jury of priests to acquit Jesus?

Early the next morning, the religious leaders bound Jesus and delivered him to Pilate, the Roman governor of the region. Pilate was responsible to Rome for preserving order in his jurisdiction. Just as he had when he stood before the high priest, Jesus did not defend himself in his trial before Pilate.

Each year during the Passover festival Pilate would release any prisoner the crowd asked for. When the crowd asked Pilate to set a prisoner free, he asked them, *"Do you want me to release to you the king of the Jews?"* Pilate knew the only reason the chief priests had turned Jesus over to him was because they were jealous of Jesus. But the chief priests agitated the crowd to call for Pilate to release Barabbas, a Jewish nationalist convicted of committing a murder during a riot.

"What shall I do, then, with the one you call the king of the Jews?" Pilate asked them.

"Crucify him!" they shouted.

"Why? What crime has he committed?" asked Pilate.

But they shouted all the louder, "Crucify him!"

Wanting to satisfy the crowd, Pilate released Barabbas to them. He had Jesus flogged, and handed him over to be crucified.

[Mark 15:1–15]

> If you were granted an interview with Pilate in the days following Jesus' trial, what questions would you ask him?

Soldiers were charged with carrying out the crucifixion of Jesus. They knelt before him in mock homage and offered him sarcastic salutes *(Hail, King of the Jews!)*. They beat him, spat on him, clothed him in a purple cloak and put a crown of thorns of his head. When they'd finished attempting to humiliate him, they stripped him of the cloak and put his own clothes back on him. They then led him out of town to crucify him and forced a passer-by, Simon of Cyrene, to carry his cross.

They led Jesus outside of Jerusalem to a place called Golgotha to crucify him. They offered him wine mixed with the herb myrrh as an anesthetic, but he refused to drink it. They nailed him to the cross at the third hour of the day — 9 a.m.

They divided his clothes among them and cast lots to decide while each soldier would take. They posted the charge against him — *The King of the Jews* — on the cross: And they crucified two robbers on either side of him.

Passerby and religious leaders mocked him and hurled insults at him. By mid-day, darkness cloaked the land. At 3 o'clock (the ninth hour) Jesus cried out in anguish: *"My God, my God, why have you forsaken me?"*

After being taunted with a sponge full of vinegar to drink, with a loud cry, Jesus breathed his last. At that moment, the curtain of the temple was torn in two from top to bottom.

A Roman military commander who had witnessed Jesus' death, said, *"Surely this man was the Son of God!"*

[Mark 15:16–39]

- If you asked Jesus what he meant when he said that God had forsaken him, what do you think his answer would be?

- What do you think moved the Roman military commander to declare that Jesus must be the Son of God?

- People responded to the crucifixion of Jesus in various ways — and still do today. What do you think accounts for the differences?

- And more importantly — how do you respond to his crucifixion?

FOR FURTHER DISCUSSION OR PERSONAL REFLECTION:

[MARK 14:53-65]
Did Jesus get a fair trial?

[MARK 15:1-15]
How do you explain the role the crowd played in the drama of the arrest and conviction of Jesus?

How susceptible are you to a "mob mentality"? Have you ever been caught up in an event of great peer pressure? If so, how did you respond?

[MARK 15:16-39]
The religious leaders suggested that if Jesus were the Christ, the Messiah they'd been waiting for, he would come down from the cross and save himself. What would you say to the religious leaders in response to this assumption? What do the religious leaders' words imply about their understanding of the Messiah?

SESSION 11

HOW CAN AN EMPTY TOMB CONTAIN AN INVITATION?

Mark 15:40–Mark 16:20

The story of Jesus didn't end the day he died. If it had, he would be remembered as a dynamic teacher, a compassionate healer, or a renegade unafraid to speak truth to power.

Instead, our journey with Jesus takes us to the place where his followers claim that the greatest enemy of the human race was vanquished once for all: to an empty tomb at sunrise.

The women who'd followed Jesus everywhere — Mary Magdalene, Mary the mother of James the younger and Joses, and Salome — witnessed Jesus' crucifixion from a distance.

These same women accompanied Joseph of Arimethea, a respected member of the religious leadership, as he brought Jesus' body to a tomb he owned. After wrapping the body in linen, Joseph placed the body in a tomb hewn into rock, and then rolled a large millstone over the tomb's opening before the start of the Jewish Sabbath.

Just after sunrise on the first day of the week, after the Sabbath ended, the women headed to the tomb to prepare Jesus' body for its final burial. They wondered aloud how they'd move the heavy millstone blocking the entrance to the tomb.

But when they looked up, they saw that the stone, which was very large, had been rolled away. As they entered the tomb, they saw a young man dressed in a white robe sitting on the right side, and they were alarmed.

"Don't be alarmed," he said. *"You are looking for Jesus the Nazarene, who was crucified. He has risen! He is not here. See the place where they laid him. But go, tell his disciples and Peter, 'He is going ahead of you into Galilee. There you will see him, just as he told you.'"*

Trembling and bewildered, the women went out and fled from the tomb. They said nothing to anyone, because they were afraid.

[Mark 15:40–16:8]

> - **What might be significant about who discovered the empty tomb?**
> - **Why were the women trembling, bewildered and afraid?**
> - **How does the resurrection illuminate the message Jesus gave throughout his ministry?**

Later Jesus appeared to the Eleven as they were eating; he chastised them for their lack of faith and their stubborn refusal to believe those who'd seen him after he had risen. He then charged them to spread the gospel both in word and in supernatural deed: *"Go into all the world and preach the good news to all creation. Whoever believes and is baptized will be saved, but whoever does not believe will be condemned."*

The disciples went out and preached everywhere, and the Lord worked with them and confirmed his word by the signs that accompanied it.

[Mark 16:9–20]

> - **Does it surprise you that Mark (and Peter, who was likely a source for this gospel) was so "brutally honest" as to acknowledge the "lack of faith" and "stubborn refusal to believe" on the part of those closest to Jesus?**
> - **Why do you think they would be willing to let those who whom they were sharing the gospel know this?**
> - **What is your understanding of Jesus after taking this journey? What new discoveries did you make? What new insights did you gain?**

Your journey isn't over.

Perhaps your journey with Jesus has just begun. Or maybe you've been challenged to follow him more closely than you ever have before. The empty tomb has an invitation just for you. It contains the same invitation he gave to his first friends and followers: *Follow me.* The living risen Savior of the world.

> - **How will you respond? What will be required of you to follow Jesus here and now?**

EPILOGUE

During the 11 sessions of this study, you've sampled a bit of what the first disciples experienced as they walked with Jesus through the three and a half years of his active ministry. You've had a whirlwind adventure together with those in your group. Questions have guided your time of dialog during this study. We'd like to leave you with a few more questions to consider on your own.

1. Are you willing to ask Jesus to give you a new beginning with him and transform your life?

2. Can you make following him your highest priority?

3. What would you tell someone else about what you're learning about Jesus?

4. Are you willing to share the Good News about him with others in your world?

As you continue to journey with Jesus, please remember that you are not traveling alone. He's gone ahead of you to blaze the trail, and he promises to be with you every step of the way. He promises to give a purposeful, flourishing and meaningful life now and for eternity to all who journey with him, to each person who affirms that Jesus is Lord and Savior. Moreover he has promised to provide the wisdom, the power and even the words you need to invite others to follow him, too.

If you enjoyed this study the life of Jesus as told by the Apostle Mark, you may want to study Paul's letter to the church in Rome. *LIGHTING THE WAY* is a 12-session small group exploration of the fundamentals of the Christian life during which we'll see how the Apostle Paul shines a bright light on God's "good news".

You may also want to consider studying the life of Jesus as told by the Apostle John. *TRANSFORMATION* is a 13-session small-group exploration designed to deepen your understanding of God's love and forgiveness as expressed in the life and teachings of Jesus Christ. *LIGHTING THE WAY* and *TRANSFORMATION* from Living Dialog Ministries, are available from online retailers and bookstores everywhere.

Please visit our website, www.lifesbasicquestions.com, for a place to engage some of the core questions of life. The website is designed to be a user-friendly way to dialog about the kinds of issues you encountered in your study of the Gospel of Mark. There is also a place on the website for visitors to ask their own questions, and receive a confidential response from the Living Dialog Ministry team. It's a helpful, no-cost resource you can share with others.

ABOUT US
Directors of the Living Dialog Ministries

JOHN C. (JACK) DANNEMILLER, Chairman and CEO of The Living Dialog Ministries, is the former Chair and CEO of Applied Industrial Technologies, a Fortune 1000 corporation. He is a 30-year leader of small group Bible studies, a frequent speaker at Christian Businessmen events, and a lecturer at the Weatherhead Graduate School of Business of Case Western Reserve University where he was honored with the Distinguished Alumni Award.

IRVING R. STUBBS, President Emeritus of The Living Dialog Ministries, is a minister with degrees from Davidson College and Union Theological Seminary in New York. He served in pastorates, an urban ministry, and consultant to business, media, religious, government, and professional organizations and their executives in North America, Europe, and Asia. He is the author and co-author of books, articles, and learning resources.

MICHELLE VAN LOON is the author of two books about the parables of Christ and has contributed to devotional projects. She's done a wide variety of freelance writing including plays and skits, curriculum, articles, and ghost-writing. She's been a church communications director, served on staff at Trinity International

University, and currently handles communications responsibilities on a freelance basis for a handful of small faith-based non-profits. She blogs at www.patheos.com/blogs/pilgrimsroadtrip/.

HENRY R. (HARRY) POLLARD, IV, Secretary of The Living Dialog Ministries, is Chairman, Partner, and Practicing Attorney with Parker, Pollard, Wilton & Peaden, PC of Richmond, Virginia where he has practiced law for more than 40 years. He has served as an officer and director of numerous businesses including banking, real estate, and financial entities. He is co-founder and Chairman of The Values Institute of America.

KENT E. ENGELKE, Treasurer of The Living Dialog Ministries, is a Managing Director and Chief Economic Strategist for Capitol Securities Management, a $6.1 billion asset management company, and has served as a director of several publicly traded banks and mortgage banking firms. His views on the economy and the markets are routinely solicited by major media outlets. He credits God for the words he writes daily and thanks God for courage and perseverance in overcoming obstacles.

BRIAN N. REGRUT, Executive Director of The Living Dialog Ministries, is a former public relations executive and consultant, corporate speech writer, author and lecturer serving clients in the fields of telecommunications, financial services and education. He has served in a variety of church leadership roles including preaching and teaching. He and his wife of 51 years have taught Sunday School together and have led small group Bible studies for many years.

A THOUGHT-PROVOKING EVANGELISM TOOL FOR CHURCHES AND ORGANIZATIONS

For those on a journey of discovery, finally answers to the profound questions of life. This little book has been distributed to thousands.

Available in bulk at a reasonable cost with a customized cover featuring your logo and message from your church or organization.

Join the dialog
www.lifesbasicquestions.com

For pricing email
lifesbasicquestions@outlook.com

CHECK OUT OUR OTHER SMALL GROUP EXPLORATIONS

TRANSFORMATION

is designed to lead your small group through a rewarding study of the life Jesus as related by the Apostle John.

During the 13 sessions filled with thought-provoking questions, you will engage with others in an interactive format allowing you to gain new insights into Jesus, God's son and mankind's savior.

LIGHTING THE WAY

guides groups through an exploration of the Apostle Paul's letter to the followers of Christ who lived in Rome. In this epistle, Paul lays down the principal doctrines of Christianity that have guided the Church for two millennia.

Each of the 12 sessions starts with a thought-provoking question followed by biblically accurate, narrative interspersed with questions the group can use as dialog starters.

www.ingramcontent.com/pod-product-compliance
Lightning Source LLC
Chambersburg PA
CBHW072105290426
44110CB00014B/1836